www.JonCrimes.com

How to Optimize YouTube Videos

Jon Crimes

How to Optimize YouTube Videos

Contents

Disclaimer 5
Introduction 7
Why YouTube? 12
Step 1 Keyword Research 14
    Google Keyword Planner 15
    Checking the Keyword: YouTube 20
    Checking the Keyword: Google 21
Step 2 The Video 22
    Say your Keyword in the video.......... 22
    Video File: Main Keyword 23
Step 3 Upload and Optimize 24
    Video Title 24
    Video Description............................ 25
    Secondary Keywords 28
    Video Tags...................................... 30
Step 4 Once Your Video is Uploaded 31
    Annotations 31
    Manage Subtitles and Closed Captions 35
    Ping Your Video URL......................... 37
    Play Your Video! 38

www.JonCrimes.com

Create a Related Video Playlist........... 39
Views, Comments & Thumbs Ups! 42
Summary 48
Resources.. 50
Quick Checklist................................ 52

How to Optimize YouTube Videos

Figure 1: WP Affiliate Plugin Video 9
Figure 2: GKP - New Keywords................. 16
Figure 3: GKP - Get Ideas....................... 17
Figure 4: GKP - Keyword ideas 18
Figure 5: GKP - Monthly searches 19
Figure 6: Checking Keyword on YouTube .. 20
Figure 7: Checking Keyword in Google...... 21
Figure 8: Example Video Description 27
Figure 9: Page Source and Keyword Ideas 30
Figure 10: Selecting Annotations 31
Figure 11: Video Time Bar 32
Figure 12: Creating Your Annotation 33
Figure 13: Setting Annotation End Time.... 34
Figure 14: End Annotation 35
Figure 15: Closed Captions 37
Figure 16: Using Pingler 38
Figure 17: Selecting Playlists 40
Figure 18: Selecting New Playlist 40
Figure 19: Add Videos........................... 41
Figure 20: Completed Playlist................. 42
Figure 21: Facebook (Link in Post).......... 46
Figure 22: Facebook (Link in Comments).. 46

www.JonCrimes.com

Disclaimer

Copyright © 2016 by Jon Crimes

All rights reserved. No part of this book may be reproduced or transmitted
in any form or by any means, electronic or mechanical, including photocopying, recording or by any information storage and retrieval system, without written permission from the author, except for the inclusion of brief quotations in a review.

The information presented herein represents the views of the author as of the date of publication.

Because of the rate with which conditions change, the author reserves the rights to alter and update his opinions based on the new conditions.

This product is for informational purposes only and the author does not accept any responsibilities for any liabilities resulting from the use of this information.

While every attempt has been made to verify the information provided here, the author

How to Optimize YouTube Videos

and his referrals cannot assume any responsibility for errors, inaccuracies or omissions. Any slights of people or organizations are unintentional.

www.JonCrimes.com

Introduction

This guide will help you to rank your videos on YouTube and in Google Search, quickly!

Now I'll be honest from the start, how quickly this happens does depend on you following all the steps in this book and taking into account what niche you are working in.

For example, if you're trying to rank a video in the Internet Marketing niche then you might find it needs more attention and work than if you had a video about "how to grow strawberries".

It stands to reason that the more competitive a niche is, the more effort you need to put into it to get great results.

Saying that, the steps in this guide will work for any niche providing you take that all important action!

I've found that, done right, creating and optimizing videos for YouTube and Google is one of the best ways to drive traffic to your website, blog, list and offers.

How to Optimize YouTube Videos

But it's not enough just to create hundreds of videos hoping that a few of them will really take off and go viral.

What works best is to start off with 1 video!

Do proper research into keywords for that video, produce a video which is not too short (think 4 mins +), include links and annotations which will drive traffic to your site.

Then monitor that video for the next couple of weeks to ensure its ranking well in both YouTube and Google.

If it's not, then you need to review what you've done and make changes where necessary.

Want some proof?

Ok, throughout this guide I'll be showing you a live example of a video that I've just created called 'WP Affiliate Plugin".

After 48 hours of carrying out the exact same steps I share with you in this guide the video was number 3 on YouTube for that Keyword!

Check out figure 1 and you'll see what I mean!

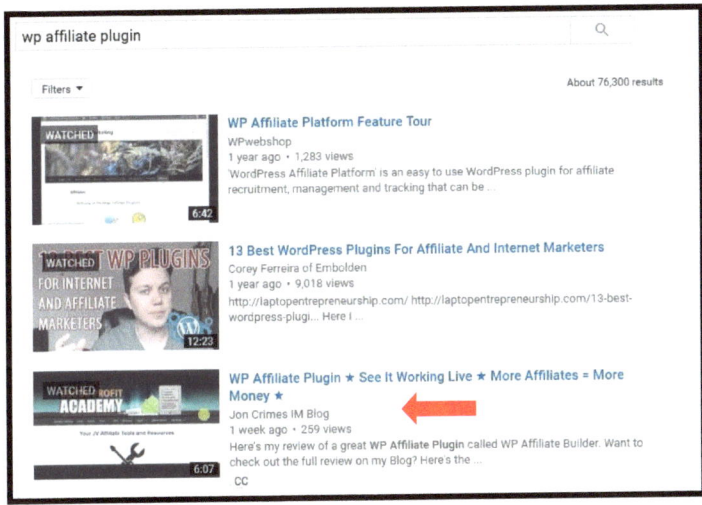

Figure 1: WP Affiliate Plugin Video

It was also on page 2 of Google search (and climbing!).

So if you follow the steps in this guide and produce a good quality video that people are going to want to watch then you can do the same.

How to Optimize YouTube Videos

Shy? You're not alone! When I first started creating videos to drive traffic I was very unsure about being in front of the camera.

Some people are natural at doing this, I'm most certainly not but I can assure you that confidence with creating videos comes with experience; you just need to make a start.

And of course, you don't need to do 'face on camera' videos at first anyway.

You can do 'over the shoulder' videos where you video capture your computer screen and speak into a microphone or even do a slideshow with some music in the background.

I'm not going to go into the technical details of video creation in this guide!

But if you want any more information on doing any of these things then I would highly recommend that you head over to YouTube and do a search for "how to record your computer screen" or "how to create a slideshow and turn into video".

www.JonCrimes.com

In fact if you're unsure of anything to do with video creation, start asking the questions on YouTube.

Finally, if you need any help or if you've got any comments about this guide then please don't hesitate to get in touch; you can find my contact details on my blog.

Happy video ranking.

Jon Crimes

[Internet Marketing Made Easy Blog](http://www.joncrimes.com/blog/)

http://www.joncrimes.com/blog/

How to Optimize YouTube Videos

Why YouTube?

Did I mention traffic?

YouTube brings me most of my traffic by a long way and providing you optimize you videos correctly, this traffic can be pretty much 'evergreen' and you'll see constant visitors arriving to your site from the link in your videos for years to come!

Compare this to other forms of traffic generation (blog comments, forum posting etc.), which might have a very limited traffic generating window, then it's easy to see why YouTube can quickly become your first choice.

Another big factor is Google!

Google bought YouTube in 2006 and it's very difficult to see this search engine disappearing any time soon.

YouTube is now the second largest search engine after, you guessed it, its parent company Google and it's reported that there's around 50,000 videos being viewed on YouTube, around the world, every second!

50,000 videos every second! That is truly staggering.

So what better way to get free traffic than to play the Google and YouTube game and the real beauty of this is that you don't need to optimize for both 'search engines'. You just need to optimize your video for YouTube and it will automatically be ranked by Google in return.

Let's start to do this!

How to Optimize YouTube Videos

Step 1
Keyword Research

This is the most important step in ranking your video on YouTube and Google!

You need to have a good keyword from the start which is going to be possible to rank for.

So stay away from the big popular keywords and instead focus on keywords which will still bring you decent traffic but have not been saturated with competition.

So, for your main keyword (and secondary keywords that you can 'sprinkle' into your video description!) aim for:

1. Over 100 monthly searches
2. Low exact matches on YouTube (5,000 or less)
3. Low exact matches on Google (100,000 or less)

To find these keywords, I use the 'Google Keyword Planner' and also 'Traffic Travis'.

For the purpose of this guide I'm going to show you how to find them with Googles Keyword Planner but if you're interested in finding out how to do it with Traffic Travis then use the following link:

http://www.joncrimes.com/blog/recommends-traffictravis

The free version is very good by the way!

Google Keyword Planner

So first of all, you need to get access to Googles Keyword Planner (GKP!).

To do this you need a Google AdWords account (you don't need to pay for ads or anything by the way). If you haven't already got an account then this next link will get you setup really quickly:

https://support.google.com/adwords/answer/2999770

Once your account is setup and you've got access to Googles Keyword Planner then you need to click on "Search for new keywords..." as shown in figure 2.

How to Optimize YouTube Videos

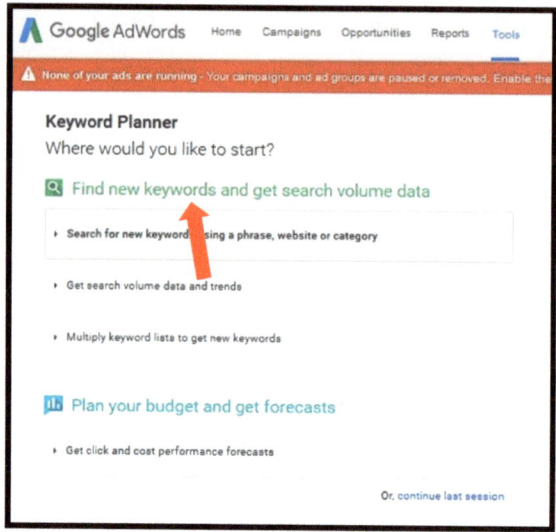

Figure 2: GKP - New Keywords

Now we need to enter an idea into the 'Your product or service' box.

For this example, I'm creating a video about a product called 'WP Affiliate Builder'.

So, I'm going to put this in the top box, check that I'm happy with my 'Targeting' options and click 'Get ideas', as shown in figure 3.

www.JonCrimes.com

Note:

With this example I'm happy to do a search for this keyword idea targeting 'All locations' because of the nature of the product.

Your example might be different and if for instance you're creating a video which is more targeted to the USA or UK, then you need to change your targeting information to reflect that.

To do this, just click on the editing 'pencil' symbol to the right of whatever you need to change!

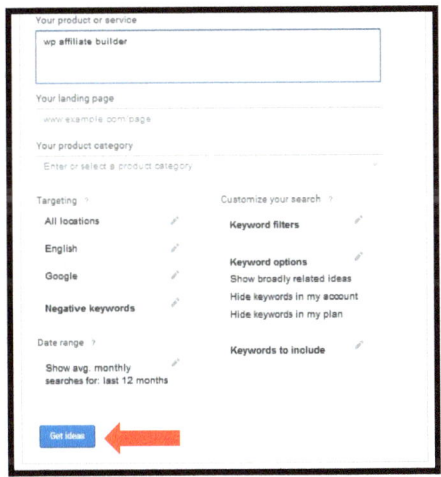

Figure 3: GKP - Get Ideas

How to Optimize YouTube Videos

The next screen you come to automatically displays the 'Ad group ideas' section. You need to click on the 'Keyword ideas' tab just below the monthly graphs and then we get to figure 4!

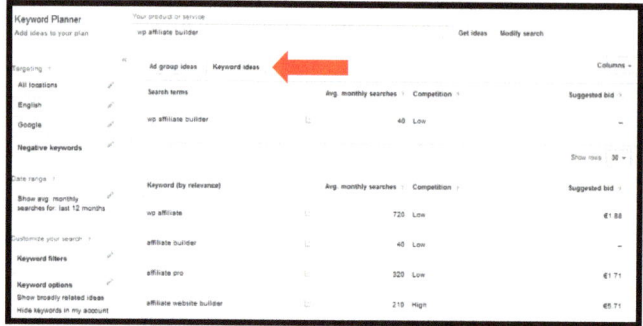

Figure 4: GKP - Keyword ideas

Here you see 2 boxes. The upper box contains our idea (product/service) keyword and the lower box is giving us other keyword ideas from Google searches.

For this example our original keyword idea 'WP Affiliate Builder' only returns 40 searches/month so we're going to ignore that one and concentrate on the lower box.

Now click on the 'Avg. monthly searches' section and this will organize the results into highest first.

www.JonCrimes.com

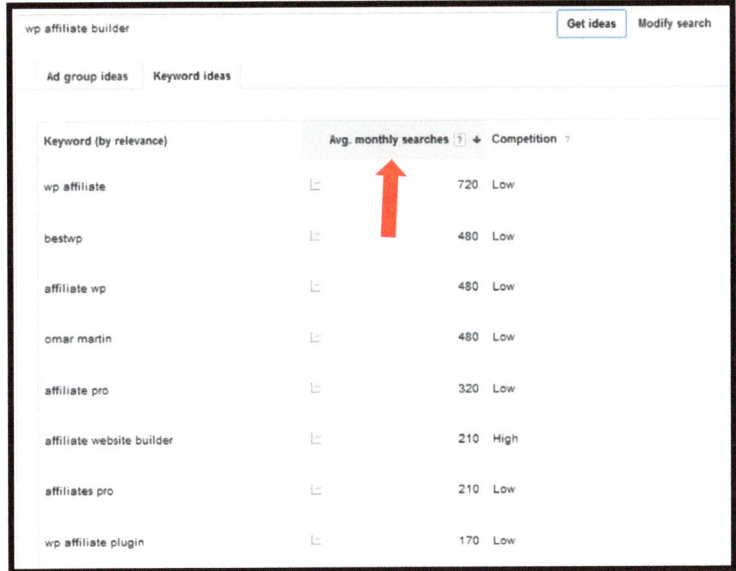

Figure 5: GKP - Monthly searches

Looking at this list of keywords and their monthly searches one particular keyword has caught my eye and that's 'WP Affiliate Plugin'.

Ok, it's only got 170 monthly searches but you've got to think of it in terms of being able to rank for a keyword and getting a good share of that traffic!

If there was a keyword there with 1000 monthly searches then I would of course investigate it further but there would be a

How to Optimize YouTube Videos

good chance that the competition would be too high.

Let's see if WP Affiliate Plugin meets the other criteria that we set earlier?

Checking the Keyword: YouTube

Now we head over to YouTube and check to see if the main Keyword we found on Google Keyword Planner meets the criteria of having 5,000 or less 'exact' matches.

To do this we type the keyword into YouTube search with quotation marks as shown in figure 6:

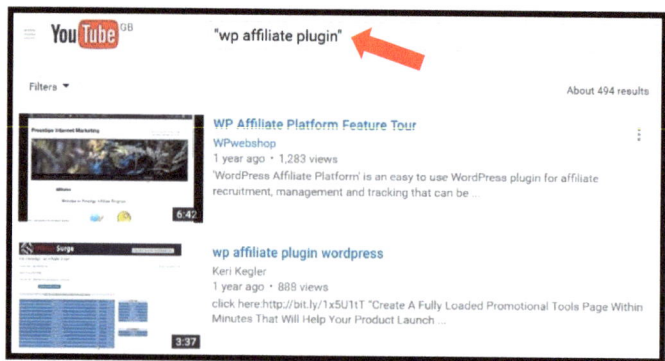

Figure 6: Checking Keyword on YouTube

We can see that the exact match for this keyword gives us about 494 search results which is a 'green light' to continue onto the next step!

Checking the Keyword: Google

Now we head over to Google Search and again do a search for the keyword using quotation marks and see if it meets our criteria of 100,000 or less exact matches.

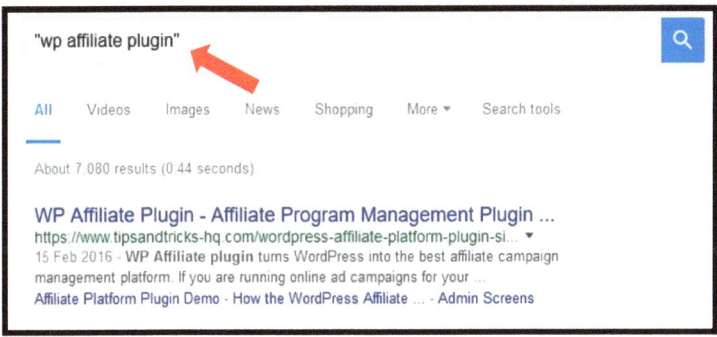

Figure 7: Checking Keyword in Google

Figure 7 shows us that the exact match for this keyword (remember to use quotation marks!) is slightly over 7,000.

So for my video, I'm going to choose 'WP Affiliate Plugin' as the main keyword.

How to Optimize YouTube Videos

Step 2
The Video

As I said in the introduction, this guide isn't about how to create a video and if you need any help with that then please do some research on YouTube where you'll find a ton of videos about how to this.

However, here are 2 tips which you might want to consider which I believe do have an effect on how well your video is ranked on YouTube (and Google!).

Say your Keyword in the video

YouTube transcribes your video automatically which can help people with hearing disabilities and there's a lot of established 'YouTubers' who state that's it's beneficial for ranking to make sure that your main keyword is in this video transcript at the beginning and end of the video.

Of course, no-one quite knows the full ranking formula with YouTube but because this doesn't take any effort to do once you get into the habit of doing it, it's worth including as part of your optimization routine!

So what I do is make sure I clearly say the main Keyword, in this case 'WP Affiliate Plugin' in the first 10 seconds of the video and then again in the last 10 seconds of the video.

Easy to do!

Video File: Main Keyword

This is another tip that draws controversy on the internet but again it's another very quick action which a lot of people on YouTube are doing.

Once you've created your Video, save the filename of that video with your main keyword.

So my video will be called **WP Affiliate Plugin.mp4**

How to Optimize YouTube Videos

Step 3
Upload and Optimize

Now you can upload your video to YouTube and whilst it's doing that you can get to work on optimizing that video to get the best ranking possible.

Video Title

This should have your main keyword in it (preferably right at the beginning) and it should be something catchy. For my video the title is going to be:

[WP Affiliate Plugin★See It Working Live★ More Affiliates = More Money★](#)

Now the stars are optional!

There's many ways in which you can stand out from the crowd and my advice would be to have a good look at how other people are doing it with their video descriptions, especially the videos which are getting hundreds or thousands of views, comments and thumbs ups!

But you can see from my video title, it stands out, the main keyword leads the title

www.JonCrimes.com

and there's a bit of intrigue there for anyone who actually wants to see what this plugin can do 'live'!

Video Description

Make your video description worth reading!

I like to treat this as a mini blog post. Aim for at least 200 words and have your main keyword in the first and last sentence and where possible a few times throughout the description.

Just don't make it spammy.

Also, make sure you include appropriate links that might interest whoever's reading the description.

For my video description I've got links to:

- The blog post which has the full review
- The 'Subscribe to my channel'
- The video itself

Figure 8 shows the description for my video.

How to Optimize YouTube Videos

Here's my review of a great WP Affiliate Plugin called WP Affiliate Builder.

Want to check out the full review on my Blog? Here's the link: http://www.joncrimes.com/blog/wpaffiliatebuilder

I've actually used this with my new product and have to say it's spot on if you want to make email swipes, banners and more which are very easy for your Joint Venture Affiliates to use in their promotions to their customers and subscribers.

WP Affiliate builder is the most comprehensive WP Affiliate Plugin Available on the market today because of how easy it is to use, and how you can create high converting affiliate sites easily and push out these pages lightning quick rather than hiring expensive designers.

One of the great things about this WP Affiliate Plugin is that you actually install it in WordPress and then create all your pages direct from the WordPress dashboard. It's super easy to do and is suitable for beginners and the more experienced!

www.JonCrimes.com

> There's also more about this product and how to attract Joint Venture Partners in my latest blog post. Just follow the link below:
>
> WP Affiliate Builder Review Blog Post:
>
> http://www.joncrimes.com/blog/wpaffiliatebuilder
>
> Subscribe to my channel:
>
> https://www.youtube.com/channel/UCbAZt4Y37HEUuUM7zSi0gKA
>
> Link to this video:
>
> https://youtu.be/-55DhGerzzA

Figure 8: Example Video Description

Important note:

I see a lot of YouTubers still putting a list of their video tags in their description! I don't do this now after reading horror stories about videos being removed and accounts being suspended.

My advice to you is to scatter your keywords wherever possible in your description text but make it readable and never just list a bunch of keywords.

It is definitely something YouTube (and probably Google?) are thinking about so just be aware.

This help article from YouTube makes it quite clear (worth a quick read!):

https://support.google.com/youtube/answer/2801973

Secondary Keywords

So where do we get secondary keywords from? Let me explain.

A few of these I found when we did the original Google Keyword Planner research for the main keyword but the majority I grabbed straight from YouTube!

Now this is a bit sneaky so don't tell everyone but there is a way in which you can see what keywords some of the high ranking videos are using.

Type your main keyword into YouTube and see what the top ranking videos (the ones with the most views and activity) are using in their title and descriptions.

This gives you some great ideas for secondary keywords to use in your description and tags.

There is also another way! Find a video by typing in your main keyword and load that video onto your screen.

Then look at the page source code for that page. I'm using Firefox as my web browser so for me I select '*Tools-Web Developer-Page source*' from my browser top menu.

For Internet Explorer it's: '*View – Source*' from your browsers menu.

Note: You'll have to do a search on YouTube or Google if you're using any other browser software to find out how to do view the page source!

Then, take a look at the video tags in this page source!

Figure 9 shows you the sort of thing you should be looking out for!

How to Optimize YouTube Videos

```
<meta property="og:video:tag" content="wp affiliate plugin">
<meta property="og:video:tag" content="wp affiliate builder">
<meta property="og:video:tag" content="wp affiliate builder review">
<meta property="og:video:tag" content="wp affiliate builder reviews">
<meta property="og:video:tag" content="wp affiliate builder omar martin">
<meta property="og:video:tag" content="buy wp affiliate builder">
<meta property="og:video:tag" content="purchase wp affiliate builder">
<meta property="og:video:tag" content="wp affiliate builder software">
<meta property="og:video:tag" content="wp affiliate builder pro">
<meta property="og:video:tag" content="affiliate plugin">
```

Figure 9: Page Source and Keyword Ideas

Figure 9 is the page source from my video example and you can see my video tags (keywords!) listed there.

Now I'm not saying copy someone else's keywords blindly but if their video is doing well then it's worth examining what keywords they're using.

Video Tags

That brings us very nicely to entering your own Video Tags.

Just below the description for the video you want to enter your keywords (or tags as YouTube calls them!).

Start off with your main keyword and then enter the secondary ones that you found.

That's it, now's a good time to save your work (click on 'Save Changes').

www.JonCrimes.com

Step 4
Once Your Video is Uploaded

Once you've completed step 3 and your video is fully uploaded there's some more great things that we can do to further optimize our video.

Annotations

Make sure you're on your YouTube Video Manager and you can see 'Info and Settings', 'Enhancements' etc. just above your video.

Then click on 'Annotations', as shown in figure 10.

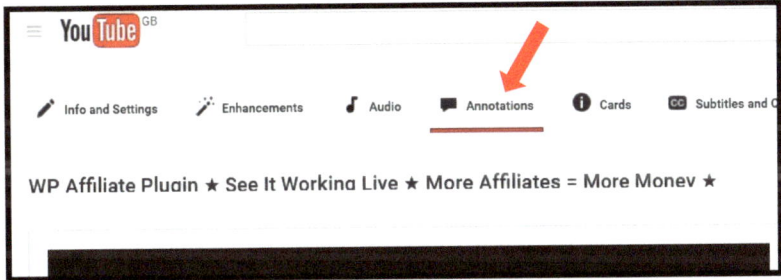

Figure 10: Selecting Annotations

What we want to do here is add an annotation in the first 10 seconds of the video which mentions your main keyword.

How to Optimize YouTube Videos

So do to this, move the time bar to the beginning of your video as shown in figure 11.

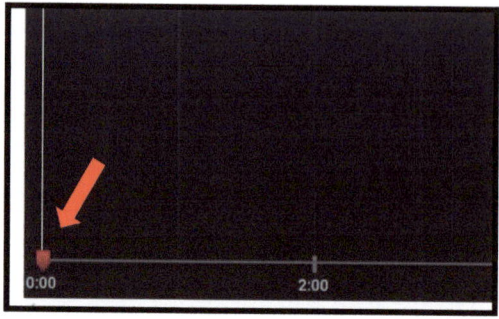

Figure 11: Video Time Bar

Then click on 'Add annotation' just to the right of your video and select 'Note'.

In the 'Note' box enter some text which includes your main keyword. For this example I'm using "Full WP Affiliate Plugin Review Here", and then customize the text and colours to suit!

You'll see your 'Note' caption pop up on your video screen and you can simply drag and drop this anywhere you want on the screen using your mouse (left-click button!). You'll also notice 4 squares around your note, these are so you can expand the box and

www.JonCrimes.com

sometimes you need to do this to make all your text visible!

Have a look at my example in figure 12.

Figure 12: Creating Your Annotation

Now, you need to change the amount of time that this annotation is visible for!

For optimization purposes we just want to have it visible for the first 10 seconds so you can either adjust the 'End' time below where you edit the text font for your note or manually go to the time bar and drag the right-hand side of the red box to the desired end time.

Figure 13 shows me setting 10 seconds as the 'End' time for this annotation.

Now do the same for the last 10 seconds of the video.

How to Optimize YouTube Videos

You can use the same text for this or do something a bit different to help to get interaction with your video.

I'm going to say "↓ Liked this WP Affiliate Plugin Review? Leave Your Comments Below ↓"

Even having something like little arrows in the text does seem to drive a bit more interaction.

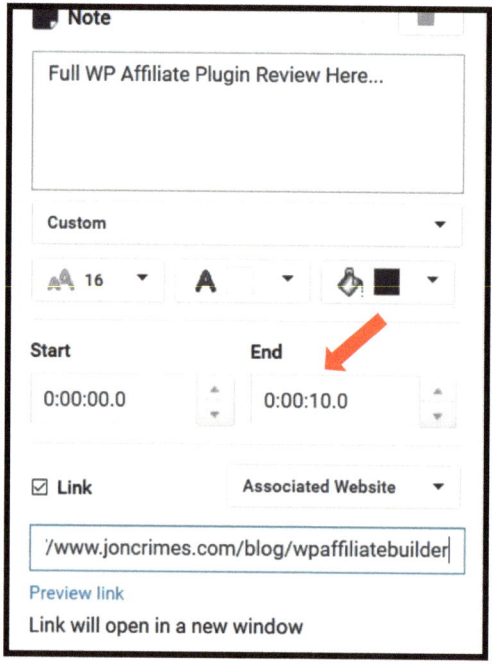

Figure 13: Setting Annotation End Time

34

www.JonCrimes.com

Here's a great link where you can simply copy and paste 'Unicode' arrows into your text:

http://xahlee.info/comp/unicode_arrows.html

Figure 14 shows my End Annotation.

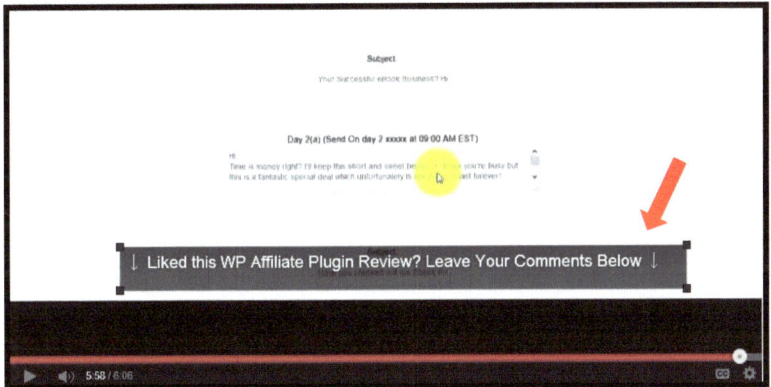

Figure 14: End Annotation

Manage Subtitles and Closed Captions

This is a great little tip which can enhance the optimization of your video.

From the Video Manager menu for your video, click on 'Subtitles and CC' and then

How to Optimize YouTube Videos

look to the right-hand of your video and you should see your published subtitles file.

Click on this file and then click on 'Edit' at the bottom of the text, you want to make sure that where you mention your main keyword in the video, YouTube has interpreted it properly!

If not, edit the text to reflect your main keyword.

When you've done this click 'Publish edits' and then delete your original Closed Caption file which has 'Automatic' after it.

Your manually changed file should now be what is displayed to anyone when they click on the 'CC' button in the bottom right-hand corner of your video.

You can see an example in figure 15.

www.JonCrimes.com

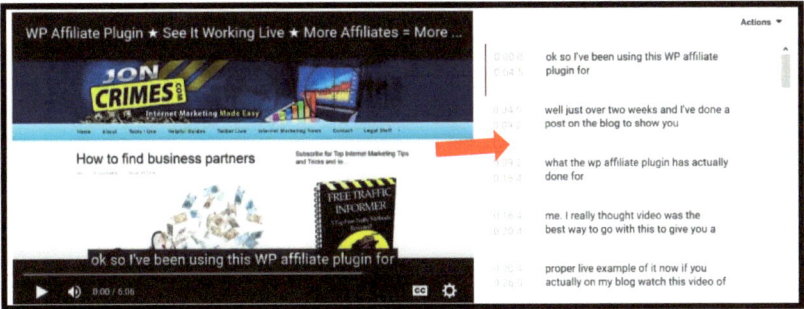

Figure 15: Closed Captions

Ping Your Video URL

Now is a great time to make the world aware of your video!

For this I use a free service called Pingler.

https://pingler.com/

So:

1. Put your main keyword in the title
2. Paste in the URL of your video (you can find this on your 'Info and Settings' page for your video)
3. Choose a suitable category (I'm going to choose 'Internet & Online' for my example)
4. Complete the 'Captcha code' and…
5. Click the 'Ping' button!

How to Optimize YouTube Videos

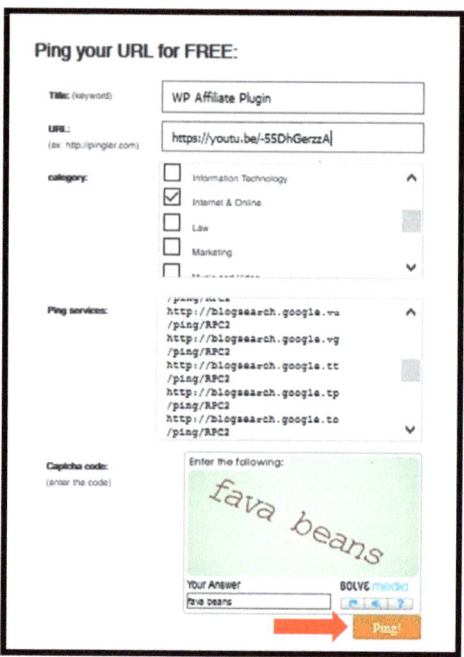

Figure 16: Using Pingler

Once you do this you'll be taken to a new page and within a few minutes your URL will be pinged to the search engines.

Play Your Video!

This is a quick and easy way to start the 'view' counter for your video and all you need to do is copy your video URL and open it in a few windows in your browser and let that video play to the end in all those windows!

Tip: make sure to mute all these videos!

By doing this you're giving your video a boost and getting it off the '0 views' mark. Doesn't take long and if you just remember to mute them then you can leave the videos playing and close down the windows later.

Create a Related Video Playlist

This is another quick and easy way to help with your video ranking.

Create a new playlist, using your main keyword as the title for this playlist and add related videos on YouTube to this list.

This is how you do this:

1. Click on your 'Video Manager' and then click on 'Playlists' in the dropdown menu

How to Optimize YouTube Videos

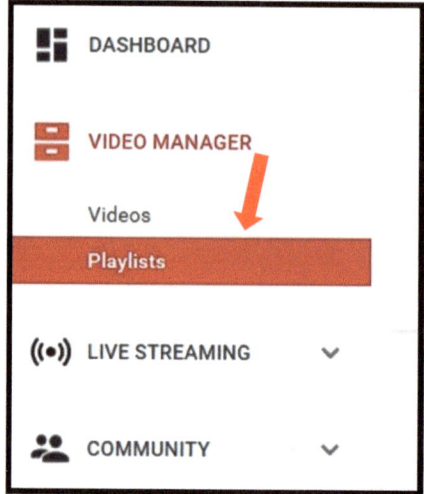

Figure 17: Selecting Playlists

2. Now click on 'New playlist'

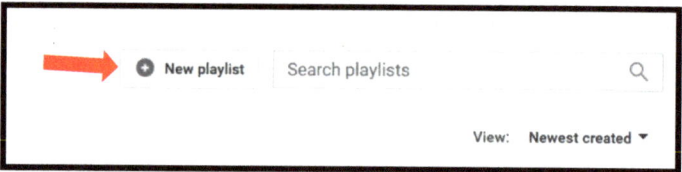

Figure 18: Selecting New Playlist

3. Enter your main keyword into where it says 'Playlist Title' and click 'Create'
4. Now click on 'Add videos' as shown in figure 19

40

www.JonCrimes.com

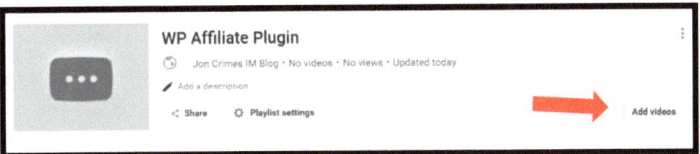

Figure 19: Add Videos

5. Then simply select the 'URL' tab and paste the URL for your video into the search box and click on the search icon.

So now your video is on this playlist you want to add some of the top ranking videos for your keyword to this playlist.

Don't worry, this won't mean people are going to watch these other videos instead of yours; it's purely for YouTube ranking purposes.

What I do now is to open YouTube in another window, do a search for my main keyword and then pick at least 5 videos for that keyword which are very active (think thousands of views!).

Click on each of these videos, copy the URL for that video and then paste it into your

How to Optimize YouTube Videos

'Add video to playlist' box on your other YouTube screen.

Figure 20 shows the playlist for my keyword 'WP Affiliate Plugin'.

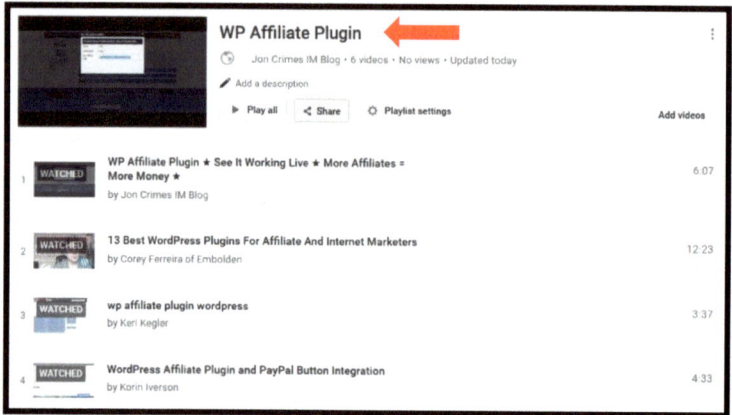

Figure 20: Completed Playlist

Views, Comments & Thumbs Ups!

One of the last things to do now is to get some social interaction for your video.

You want to get as many views, comments and thumbs ups as possible and there's 2 ways that I like to do this.

Share on social media

I personally always share my videos, straight away, on Google+, Twitter and Facebook.

www.JonCrimes.com

Try adding a catchy intro into your social media post and drive visitors to your video.

I also thoroughly recommend using Hootsuite.

https://hootsuite.com/

With this service you can manage all your social media accounts in one dashboard, type just one message and send it everywhere!

Save loads of time and the free version is great.

Facebook Video Syndication Groups
With these groups you can exchange comments, views and thumbs up with like-minded video creators!

Here are 3 video syndication groups that I thoroughly recommend joining and there's a lot more out there as well!

https://www.facebook.com/groups/269030833256792/

https://www.facebook.com/groups/155093337967986/

How to Optimize YouTube Videos

https://www.facebook.com/groups/reviewvideos/

Backlinks

A few years ago throwing thousands of poor quality backlinks at your video (and your website for that matter!) worked wonders in getting your video ranked quickly on YouTube and in the search engines.

That's not the case today!

Here's what I do to generate backlinks to my videos:

1. Social media! If you've already followed the earlier step and shared your video on social media then that's a good start to get your first decent backlinks. Now if you're particularly active on any of the social media platforms, Facebook for instance, then it's also a great idea to drive some further discussion and interaction about your video on that platform.

    With my example video, WP Affiliate Plugin, I'm going to share this on all the Internet Marketing Facebook Groups that I'm a member of.

Quick tip here, mix up your Facebook posts a bit!

What I mean by that is your post gets treated differently by Facebook depending on whether you include a link in that post or not (Facebook is not a big fan on links that are not part of its advertising program!).

At the same time, some people love to see a link attached to the post and something that is easily clickable.

My answer to this is to do 50/50. Some of the groups get a link in the post itself whilst the other half gets a link in the comments for that post. Seems to work quite nicely, check out what I mean in figures 21 & 22.

How to Optimize YouTube Videos

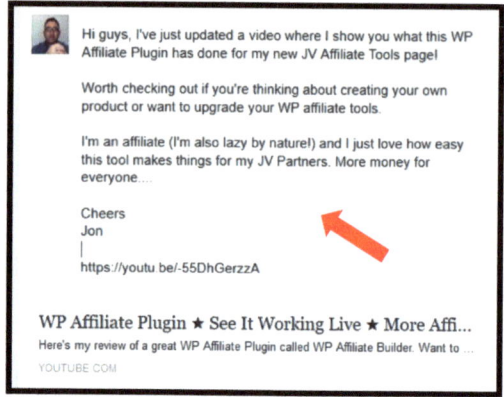

Figure 21: Facebook (Link in Post)

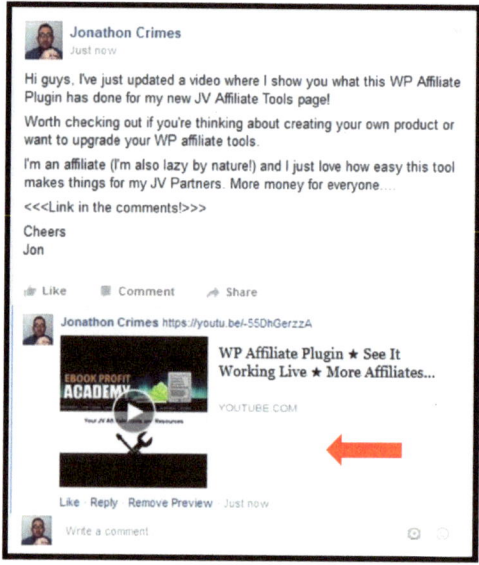

Figure 22: Facebook (Link in Comments)

2. Fiverr

The other way in which I get backlinks to my video is to use the services of Fiverr.

Now you've got to be careful here and not choose someone who's just going to send 1000's of very poor quality backlinks to your video but there are some good freelancers on this site.

Here's 3 Fiverr Sellers that I can thoroughly recommend you check out:

https://uk.fiverr.com/creative94

https://uk.fiverr.com/ytviews4you

https://uk.fiverr.com/youngceaser

Of course, Fiverr sellers do come and go but these 3 sellers have been established on Fiverr for a long time and shouldn't be disappearing any time soon!

You can also jump onto Fiverr and do a search yourself but be careful to choose a top rated (or level two!) seller and always have a good look at their feedback but parting with your $5!

How to Optimize YouTube Videos

Summary

I really hope that this guide has given you a good idea about how to get your videos ranking well on YouTube and in Google search?

It does take a bit of time do carry out all the steps in this book but believe me, this is time well spent.

I know lots of people who throw up 100's of videos in the hope of one becoming successful on YouTube. Some people get lucky but there's always the chance that just around the corner someone else is going to release a video, with your keyword, and they're going to do it properly!

Guess whose video will be on top in a weeks' time?

It might also help to make yourself a checklist so you can summarize the steps for yourself on one page?

In fact, I've already done that for you at the end of the book!

www.JonCrimes.com

Also, please don't forget to monitor your videos rank on YouTube. Sometimes a little tweak to your description or simply just going over it again with a fresh brain can produce great results.

And if you get really stuck, read through this guide again, check out what the top videos look like for your keyword or give me a shout!

You can do that by heading over to my Internet Marketing Made Easy Blog!

To your video success.

Cheers

Jon Crimes

www.joncrimes.com/blog

How to Optimize YouTube Videos

Resources

Internet Marketing Made Easy Blog

http://www.joncrimes.com/blog/

Traffic Travis

http://www.joncrimes.com/blog/recommends-traffictravis

Google Keyword Planner Guide

https://support.google.com/adwords/answer/2999770

YouTube – Spam Guide

https://support.google.com/youtube/answer/2801973

Unicode Symbols

http://xahlee.info/comp/unicode_arrows.html

URL Ping Service

https://pingler.com/

Social Media Management

www.JonCrimes.com

https://hootsuite.com/

Facebook Video Syndication Groups

https://www.facebook.com/groups/269030833256792/

https://www.facebook.com/groups/155093337967986/

https://www.facebook.com/groups/reviewvideos/

Fiverr Video Backlink Sellers

https://uk.fiverr.com/creative94

https://uk.fiverr.com/ytviews4you

https://uk.fiverr.com/youngceaser

How to Optimize YouTube Videos

Quick Checklist

- ☐ Choose a subject keyword for your video
- ☐ Insert this subject keyword into Google Keyword Planner and find a suitable main keyword that has over 100 monthly searches
- ☐ Check your main keyword on YouTube. Use quotation marks to find the exact matches for this keyword, ensure it has less than 5,000 "exact" matches
- ☐ Check your keyword in Google search. Use quotation marks again to find exact matches. Ensure less than 100,000 exact matches
- ☐ Make a short list of secondary keywords by using your research on Google Keyword Planner and by analysing top videos for your main keyword on YouTube
- ☐ When producing your video, say your main keyword in the first and last 10 seconds of the video
- ☐ When your video is finished, save using your main keyword as the videos filename

www.JonCrimes.com

- ☐ Video title. Include your main keyword in the title and make the title catchy!
- ☐ Video description. At least 200 words. Put main keyword in first and last sentence. Don't stuff keywords!
- ☐ Video description. Include links to your site
- ☐ Video description. Add secondary keywords where possible in the content but again, don't stuff them in! Make your description very reader friendly
- ☐ Video tags. Put your main keyword first followed by your secondary keywords.
- ☐ Remember to save your changes!
- ☐ Annotations. Add an annotation to the first 10 secs of your video which includes your main keyword
- ☐ Annotations. Have a call to action at the end of the video
- ☐ Subtitles and closed captions. Ensure that your closed caption file has your main keyword transcribed correctly (refer to guide)
- ☐ Ping your video URL. Head over to https://pingler.com/

How to Optimize YouTube Videos

- ☐ Open and play your video (to the end!) in 5 separate windows (make sure you mute the videos)
- ☐ Create a related video playlist. Ensure your video is number 1 in the playlist
- ☐ Share on social media to get views, comments and thumbs up
- ☐ Share and interact on Facebook Video Syndication Groups
- ☐ Get backlinks to your video. Social media and Fiverr (refer to guide!)

www.ingramcontent.com/pod-product-compliance
Lightning Source LLC
Chambersburg PA
CBHW040900180526
45159CB00001B/472